Marjorie Caygill

The British Museum Reading Room

Published for The Trustees
of The British Museum

The British Museum Reading Room

Will you be kind enough to have some books of superstitions, love, marriage, birth, weather, flowers, cats, dress, Christmas, New Year, Midsummer, All Hallows, illness, etc., ready for me for tomorrow (Sat.) morn?

Letter from a lady to the Superintendent of the British Museum Reading Room (1923)

The Reading Room of the British Museum is unique. Here for almost 150 years scholars and revolutionaries, writers, poets and musicians, students and copyists, and a sprinkling of eccentrics came to consult the greatest library in the world. The novelist Virginia Woolf wrote: 'There is in the British Museum an enormous mind... hoarded beyond the power of any single mind to possess it. Nevertheless... one can't help thinking how one might come with a notebook, sit at a desk, and read it all through.' (*Jacob's Room*, 1922)

Access to this incomparable library was not the preserve of the rich and influential alone. The creator of the Reading Room, Antonio Panizzi, set out his philosophy for it in 1836: 'I want a poor student to have the same means of indulging his learned curiosity, of following his rational pursuits, of consulting the same authorities, of fathoming the most intricate inquiry as the richest man in the kingdom, as far as books go, and I contend that the Government is bound to give him the most liberal and unlimited assistance in this respect.'

Karl Marx came here daily for almost 30 years, researching and writing, refining his theory of class struggle. A generation later, Lenin, when not attending political meetings or following his pastime of riding on the top deck of London buses, also read and researched, awaiting the opportunity to put Marx's theories into practice.

In addition to the real inhabitants of the room, there are many fictional characters. Perhaps the most poignant is the doomed poet Enoch Soames, who, in a piece by Max Beerbohm, sells his soul to the devil on 3 June 1897 for the opportunity to visit the Reading Room a century hence to admire his entries in the *Catalogue*, only to find that he is dismissed in a few lines as 'an imaginary character and a third-rate poet'. By then it is too late and the devil returns in 1897 to claim his part of the bargain.

Until recently the Reading Room, was open only to holders of readers' tickets who were able to convince the Library Clerks that their research merited admission. Today this magnificent room welcomes all members of the public.

Previous page: The Reading Room in 1875. In the foreground is the area, rows K to P, in which Karl Marx worked. Photograph by Frederic York

Earlier reading rooms

Day by day readers multiplied; year by year collections, especially of printed books, spread at an extraordinary rate… not only the shelves were completely filled, but the floors of the libraries were crowded in every direction

A Handbook for Readers at the British Museum (1866)

The British Museum was founded by Act of Parliament in 1753 to house the multifarious collections of the eminent physician Sir Hans Sloane (1660–1753), which included a choice library, and the manuscripts amassed by the Cotton and Harley families. In 1754, using public lottery money, the Museum acquired Montagu House, a 17th-century mansion on the site of the present Museum building. In 1757 King George II donated the 'Old Royal Library' of the sovereigns of England and with it the privilege of 'copyright deposit', that is, the right to a copy of every printed work published in the country. This gift, and others which were to follow, ensured that the library would expand indefinitely.

On 15 January 1759 the Museum opened to the public. From the outset a 'damp and dark' reading room was provided, a corner room in the south-west basement, furnished by 20 chairs and an oak table covered with green baize, the walls gloomily lined with stuffed birds.

The first reading room soon proved inadequate and was succeeded by others, all of which were outgrown. In 1823, following the gift by King George IV of his father's library of some 65,000 books and 800 volumes of unbound pamphlets, a new building for the Museum designed by Sir Robert Smirke (1780–1867) was begun. This included a new reading room which came into use in 1838 – two rooms in the north-east corner (now much altered and occupied by the Mexican Gallery and the Chase Manhattan Gallery of North America). By the time the new reading room was finished the collection of printed books amounted to 230,000 volumes and there was virtually no room for expansion. The 1838 rooms were therefore replaced in 1857 by the round Reading Room which we see today.

The 1838 Reading Room designed by Sir Robert Smirke which was replaced by the round Reading Room of 1857. Watercolour by Thomas Hosmer Shepherd

Antonio Panizzi (1797–1879): founder of the Reading Room

At various times in his career it was alleged against Panizzi as a crime that he was a foreigner, and certainly his experiences as an Italian conspirator, though it won him the sympathy of influential English statesmen, left him in some respects at a disadvantage as compared with men who have passed through the mill of an English public school and university

The Library (2nd series, 7, 11, 1 July 1901)

Sir Anthony Panizzi, Keeper of Printed Books 1837–56, Principal Librarian 1856–66, originator of the Reading Room. Oil painting by George Frederic Watts RA

Panizzi's preliminary sketch for the Reading Room made on 18 April 1852

The man who provided the inspiration for the Reading Room and the determination to ensure that his dream was achieved was Antonio Genesio Maria Panizzi (afterwards Sir Anthony Panizzi KCB). Panizzi was born in Italy at Brescello in the Duchy of Modena, the son of a village chemist. As a young man he graduated in law, but became involved in the struggle for Italian unification and was forced to flee, under sentence of death. He arrived in England in May 1823, with no money and speaking little English. By industry and charm, through which he developed influential contacts, he became a teacher of Italian in Liverpool, then Professor of Italian at the newly founded London University. In 1831 he joined the British Museum, becoming Keeper of Printed Books in 1837, and from 1856 to 1866 Principal Librarian (head of the Museum). His friends included the Prime Ministers Palmerston, Russell and Gladstone.

Described as 'perhaps the greatest administrative librarian who has ever lived', Panizzi applied his revolutionary zeal to the Museum collections, expanding the number of books to 600,000 in 1866 (the year of his retirement). Under his successors, the library which he had modernised reached 1.5 million volumes in 1888. Panizzi drew up the 91 rules for entering books into the Museum's catalogues, later expanded but the basis of those still applied today.

A particular achievement was his insistence on the enforcement of the Copyright Acts. The Copyright Act of 1709, according to which all British publications were to be registered at Stationers Hall, London, provided that a number of privileged libraries including the Royal Library (given to the Museum in 1757), had the right to claim copies of all registered works. During the 18th century few books were registered and few claimed. Following pressure from Panizzi, in 1842, publishers were obliged to deliver volumes directly to the British Museum and in 1850 the Museum began to take legal action against those who defaulted, leading to a vast increase in the Museum's holdings. Panizzi also managed to persuade the Treasury to provide more generous grants for purchases.

Panizzi is credited with much of the design of the Reading Room from the initial concept to details such as furniture and fittings.

Sydney Smirke (1798–1877): architect of the Reading Room

The plans were drawn without outside assistance, nor could the architect suggest a single improvement
G F Barwick, *The Reading Room of the British Museum* (London, 1929)

Panizzi was an individual who tended to attract adulation and hatred in equal measure. So far as his supporters were concerned, the Reading Room was Panizzi's creation and the contribution of the architect, Sydney Smirke, was largely incidental. Smirke, with perhaps a hint of desperation, wrote to *The Times* to set the record straight:

> The facts are these: some years ago the late Professor of Architecture at King's College [William Hosking] suggested building a circular, domed hall for sculpture in the quadrangle. Some years afterwards Mr Panizzi suggested building a flat, low circular reading room in the same place. The Trustees did me the honour to consult me, and I quite approved of Mr Panizzi's suggestion, but proposed a dome and glazed vaulting, to give more air to the readers and a more architectural treatment to the interior. This grew, on maturer consideration, into the much larger dome as erected… For the arrangement and form of a great number of interior details I had the invaluable advantage of the direct instructions of the Principal Librarian… Every aesthetic merit, however, that the reading room may possess I claim as literally and exclusively my own.

Sydney Smirke had initially worked as a pupil of his brother Robert (1780–1867), who was appointed architect to the Museum in 1813. Robert was responsible for the quadrangular design of the building and the great south front, but in 1845 he was obliged to withdraw from the work on account of ill-health. On Robert's recommendation, responsibility for the completion of the Museum was taken over by his younger brother, Sydney. Sydney worked to his brother's plans but introduced some of his own designs, including the forecourt and the Front Hall with the highly coloured decorative scheme by Collman and Davis now recreated there. He was in 1860 awarded the Gold Medal of the Royal Institute of British Architects for the Reading Room.

Sydney Smirke, architect. His other works include the Carlton Club, Pall Mall (1847, 1857) and exhibition galleries for the Royal Academy at Burlington House (1866–70)

Building the Reading Room

A splendid room, but perfectly unsuited, I think, to its purpose,
and an example of reckless extravagance (having cost £150,000)
occasioned through the undue influence of a Foreigner

Diaries of Sir Frederic Madden, Keeper of Manuscripts, 21 May 1857
(Bodleian Library Ms.Eng.hist c.170)

The central courtyard of the new Museum building, designed by Sir Robert Smirke in 1823, was to have been a place where the public might promenade and admire botanical plants. However, on its completion in 1847, the collections – books, antiquities and natural history – were increasing so rapidly that the Museum was again desperately short of space.

On 18 April 1852 Antonio Panizzi, sketched a plan for a circular reading room within the courtyard. One of the Assistants in the Library, Charles Cannon, put the sketch into proper form to accompany Panizzi's report to the Museum Trustees on 5 May. The plan was then refined by Sydney Smirke.

It took two years to obtain government approval but Panizzi's influential connections ensured success. The architect Sir Charles Barry (1795–1860), asked to comment on Panizzi's plans, put forward an alternative proposal, not unreminiscent of today's Great Court but not accepted at the time, that the inner courtyard be covered over by a glass roof to provide a hall 'covered wholly with glass and laid out ornamentally with fine sculpture'.

The work was completed with amazing speed. Excavations began in May 1854, the first brick was laid in September. In January 1855 the first rib of the dome was erected. On 2 June that year the scaffolding was removed and in September the dome was covered in copper. Panizzi was said to have haunted the site exhorting the workmen 'Damn you, you shall not go till you haf finished'. Prince Albert and Queen Victoria visited the site in June 1855. Both the Prince and

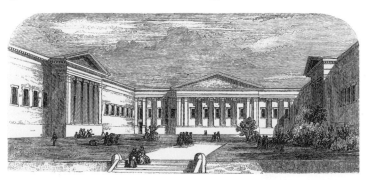

Robert Smirke's open courtyard, intended for, but never opened to, the public. Artist's impression c1845 Opposite: the Reading Room under construction. An early photograph by William Lake Price 1855

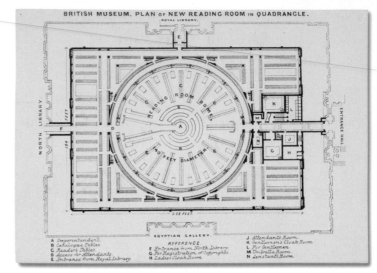

Panizzi disliked the proposed round-arched exterior windows since they did not follow the classical design of the rest of the Museum building. Following the Prince Consort's intervention a compromise was reached, with the exterior of the windows square cornered and the interior arched as today. The main contractors were Baker and Fielder of Lambeth. The total cost of the project was £150,000.

The design made innovative use of cast iron provided by a firm called 'Pontifex'. The iron ribs are each in three sections. These were not fitted together; gaps were left between the castings and filled with 'rust cement', a paste invented by William Murdoch (1754–1839) made of iron filings, sal-ammoniac and water which swelled as it set. The inner lining of the dome is of a form of papier mâché, ⅝in (15.9mm) thick, called 'fibrous slab' or patent wood, an invention registered in 1847 by C F Bielefeld and consisting of pulped paper resins, mixed with chalk.

Panizzi having said that he wished 'no inauguration or speechifying', the room was opened on 2 May 1857, at an informal champagne breakfast with ices, and bouquets for the ladies, the desks being used as tables.

Invitation to a private view of the Reading Room 5 May 1857. Thousands of visitors viewed the room in the week after its completion. The Room opened to readers on 18 May 1857

British Museum.

Admit bearer and three friends to a private view of the new building on Tuesday the 5th of May 1857 between the hours of 11 in the morning and 5 in the afternoon.

N.B. This card must be exhibited to the gate keeper at the great entrance in Great Russell Street.

'A Temple ... rich in blue, and white, and gold': decoration of the Reading Room

Today the Room is as it was when freshly painted in 1857. Panizzi would have preferred a more elaborate decorative arrangement showing branches of human creative achievement in each of the 20 bays of the dome. Such a scheme was devised by Alfred Stevens (1817–75) but the Museum's Trustees, declined to commission this project. Statues between the bays were also proposed by Panizzi, but only the plinths were constructed. In the absence of the strong coloured figures so favoured by Panizzi, Smirke advocated a generous use of gilding to compensate for the plain blue. A beneficial result, he wrote, 'would be the bringing into harmony the Dome and the walls which support it; those walls consisting wholly of books, whose bindings collectively produce a rich, warm, and somewhat deep tone, very strongly opposed to the cool light tint of the dome.'

The Reading Room was redecorated in 1907, 1951–2 and 1963–4. The 1907 redecoration, in gold and white, incorporated 19 great names in English literature (all male) under the windows. In Virginia Woolf's *Jacob's Room* (1922) the feminist Julia Hedge watches the final 'y' inserted in Lord Macaulay's name and complains 'Oh damn, why didn't they leave room for an Eliot or a Brontë?' The names did not survive the 1960s.

The Reading Room in 1907 after its redecoration by the Museum's architect Sir John Burnet. To the left an electric light globe

The 'Museum headache': heating and ventilation

To the British Museum reading room, with its courteous officials, I remain grateful; though, on the principle of making the punishment fit the crime, the party responsible for its heating arrangements ought to be suffocated

Jerome K Jerome, Dedication to *My Life and Times* (1925)

The heating and ventilation system, designed to provide air for 500 people, was in fact most ingenious and today's scheme follows similar principles. At its heart is the 'spider' a 6ft (1.8m) high air chamber beneath the Reading Room, so called because it is made up of stone ribs like a spider's web which mirror the arrangement of the desks on the floor above. The supply of fresh air reached this chamber through a tunnel connected to a shaft 60ft (18.3m) high on an inner roadway about 300ft (91.4m) to the north. The 'spider' was fitted with hot water pipes to heat the air in cold weather before it entered the Room. Air-distributing channels in each iron-framed table were connected to the spider. A tubular foot-rail still runs beneath each table and through this passed in winter a current of warm water to produce a foot-warmer. During the summer, steam pipes at the top of the dome were heated to draw out the stale air which was replaced by fresh air pumped in through the air channels in the readers' tables, emerging through a brass network at the top of each partition.

The hot water pipes in the 'spider' were in due course removed and the Room was heated by warm air pumped into this chamber. Air still enters via this route, and leaves through natural vents within the crown of the dome, although it now originates in the Great Court ventilation system.

The roof of the dome is formed into two separate spherical and concentric air-chambers extending over the whole surface; one between the external covering and the brick vaulting to prevent extremes of temperature outside making the Room too hot or too cold; the other chamber between the brick vaulting and the internal visible surface provides a channel through which stale air can escape.

'A Student', G Lawson c1890. Air was distributed from the grille above each reader's desk

**'Cold violet radiance':
lighting the
Reading Room**

*The bookworms who haunt the reading-rooms of the Museum are
on these occasions left without the means of pursuing their various
avocations. Many of this industrious and useful community leave the
beautiful dome, which in this light has a dim, lurid and somewhat
ghastly appearance, and grope their way homeward; a few more
persevering than others, having with difficulty managed to extract
the names and particulars of a few books from the catalogue, and in the
hope of the air clearing, sit with patience waiting until the painstaking
attendants have, by the aid of lanterns, carefully locked and strongly
protected with glass or crystal, provided the volumes wanted*
The Builder (July 1865)

Artificial lighting (gas or naked flames) was not permitted in the
Reading Room when it first opened. The only illumination came
from the 20 windows and the 'lantern' the glazed area at the apex
of the dome. When it became dark, or if there was heavy fog, the
room closed and the readers were sent home.

To remedy this unsatisfactory situation the Museum was one
of the first public buildings to carry out experiments into the use
of electricity. These began in February 1879 with the 'Jablochkoff'
candle'. This was later replaced by the cheaper Siemens system.

The first use of the new invention one Saturday morning in
November 1879 occasioned a rare phenomenon reported by
The Times – a murmur of spontaneous applause from the assembled
readers as 'without any apparent preparations the spacious room
was suddenly illuminated as by a magic ray of sunshine'.

In February 1880 after a piece of carbon from an open lamp
nearly ignited some papers and with them the Reading Room,
closed lamps were substituted. By October 1880 four arc lights
of 5,000 candle power each had been installed. Even then the system
had a disconcerting habit of failing altogether, leaving the readers
to be rescued by staff with lanterns. In 1893 individual 'glow lamps',
with maroon shades, were introduced to readers' tables and above

**Interior of the lantern
c1963**

15

the shelving. The arc lamps were reduced to 300 candle power each, although for some years books still had to be retrieved from the gloom of the bookstacks by attendants with lanterns.

An impression of the original lighting system is given by George Gissing, in *New Grub Street* (1891), who writes of the 'sputtering whiteness of the electric light and its ceaseless hum'.

The individual lights over the desks were removed and replaced by fluorescent lighting in the late 1940s.

The bookstacks

Free or open access can hardly be practised in so large a library as this. As it was once put, the danger would be not merely of losing the books, but also of losing readers
Arundell Esdaile, *The British Museum Library* (1946)

A labyrinth of bookstacks on several floors encircled the dome. The stacks were made of perforated iron, an ingenious method of construction which allowed natural daylight from the glass roofs to penetrate to the lowest levels. In this rectangular building in 750,000ft³ (69,675m³) of space were 3 miles (4.8km) of book cases, made up of 25 miles (40.2km) of shelving, initially with space for 1.5 million books. The adjustable shelves, supported on brass pins, for which there were 2,750,000 holes, could be altered to take various sizes of book by gradations of ⅜in (9.5mm). The Victorians estimated that if the shelves were full of books, of paper of average thickness, the leaves placed edge to edge would extend about 25,000 miles (40,000km) or more than three times the diameter of the globe.

Part of the labyrinth of bookstacks known as the 'iron library' c1949 Opposite: 'Closed week' 1933. Each year the Reading Room was refurbished and the books dusted and checked

Using the Reading Room

Having inscribed his or her name in the Register, and obtained the requisite ticket, the newly-constituted reader finds himself or herself in the centre of the Reading-room … Here one may say, is the literary mart, from which are dispensed the products of minds great, mediocre, and small; home, colonial, and foreign

A Handbook for Readers at the British Museum (1866)

Access to the Reading Room in the early part of the 19th century could be obtained only by a recommendation from a Trustee, member of staff, nobleman, Minister of State or head of a university college. Later a letter of recommendation from a person identifiable in standard reference books was accepted. Most recently, in order to relieve crowding, the Reading Room was regarded as a 'library of last resort'; readers had to satisfy the authorities that the research they were carrying out could not reasonably be accomplished elsewhere. Reader's tickets were not normally issued to those below the age of 21. Six monthly renewals were initially required, although from 1879 to 1890 life tickets were issued and in recent years one- to five-year passes were available.

Reader's ticket 1970s. The Museum retains extensive indexes of readers' names together with registers of their signatures
Opposite: Readers c 1949. The Reading Room was closed during the Second World War but suffered only slight damage during the bombing of London

Since the occasional Admissions Clerk harboured the conviction that to admit any reader who could possibly be sent elsewhere constituted a defeat, and some amassed a vast knowledge of alternative libraries, application for a ticket could be rather unsettling. Nigel Williams in *Witchcraft* (1987) described the ordeal: '"And what," said the young man behind the desk, "is your interest in the seventeenth century?" He asked this question in the tone of a hotel desk clerk, checking in a couple who have just announced they have no luggage, no means of identification, and that their married name is Smith. It was as if the British Museum was bombarded with requests from suspicious individuals eager to try any excuse or stratagem just as long as they could get in out of the cold and wrap their fingers round a juicy slice of pornography.'

(In passing, it might be noted that this would have been a forlorn hope since pornography was locked away in the so-called 'private case' to be read only under supervision and provided the Superintendent was convinced that there was a legitimate reason for permitting access.)

On arrival in the room the reader would select an empty numbered seat (these could not be booked in advance). To locate books, readers consulted the *General Catalogue of Printed Books*, stored in the semi-circular desks in the centre of the room, first printed in 1906, but initially made up of pasted handwritten slips of

paper. The *Catalogue* itself eventually consisted of around 2,300 folio volumes. It was largely arranged according to author, with each book being allotted a 'press-mark' giving its exact location in the bookstacks or, increasingly after the 1960s, at an off-site location. Titles of later publications were inserted by means of pasted slips. Panizzi's cataloguing rules, some not entirely self-evident, had to be mastered. British Museum publications, for example, could be found under 'L' for London. The *Illustrated London News* would be under 'P' for Periodical Publications. A heavy volume would be hauled out by the reader and deposited on top of the catalogue desk with a distinctive 'thunk' which echoed round the room.

The desired book or books having been located, a printed form for each item then had to be filled in and deposited at the centre desk. There were dire warnings in the 1866 *Guide* about the consequences of failing to fill in the correct seat number: 'We have heard of cases where persons… have not only waited patiently the advent of their books hour after hour, but the whole day long, and have left the Museum without seeing the books at all.'

In due course, after an hour or so, the book would arrive. Occasionally the form alone would be returned with various, often puzzling, reasons for non-delivery ticked on the back:

Badge worn by attendants in the Reading Room c 1933

> It is regretted that:
> ☐ this work was destroyed by bombing in the war; we have not been able to acquire a replacement [a reference to the destruction of the south-west bookstack by incendiary bombs during the Second World War]
> ☐ this work has been mislaid [somewhere in the 25 miles (40km) of shelving]
> ☐ this work has been missing since… [and we know when we lost it!]

Books also tended to disappear for months 'at the binders'.

Enquiries were answered at the 'keyhole' space at the north where sat the Superintendent, with a group of assistants. Books were returned to this area which is slightly raised so that the Superintendent has a clear view of the entire room and any unauthorised activities by readers.

Although all the library collections were initially consulted in the Reading Room, a series of smaller rooms was later opened elsewhere for manuscripts, maps, music, official publications, newspapers and oriental material. Rare and valuable books were for much of the 20th century consulted in the North Library (now the Wellcome Gallery). Books could not be taken outside the Reading Rooms.

Life in the Reading Room

The most interesting study in the Reading Room is the reader and it may be added that they have studied themselves and have been their own severest critics. There is hardly an infraction of the rules of the Room that has escaped comment, coupled with an urgent call on the authorities to take vigorous action against the offenders. The non-observance of silence was a constant cause of complaint, also the appropriation of more than one desk, lengthy absence from the Room while leaving a desk apparently engaged, not replacing books of reference and catalogues; using the Library steps as seats, concealing books of reference for their own use or to keep them away from others working on the same subjects, uncleanliness, intoxication, etc

G F Barwick, *The Reading Room of the British Museum* (1929)

Working in the Reading Room was an unforgettable experience. A reader in 1917 described the soft, dim light that prevailed even on a sunny morning, the peculiar odour that seemed to be compounded of leather, cork-carpet, and damp overcoats. Samuel Butler likened the readers consulting shelved books to 'wasps flying up and down an apricot tree'. The sounds were distinctive – a noise of books banging, feet walking about, and 'the endless turning of the pages of the central catalogues, like the sound of leaves swished by a gardener's broom'. Virginia Woolf remarked in *Jacob's Room*: 'Nobody laughed in the reading-room. There were shiftings, murmurings, apologetic sneezes, and sudden unashamed devastating coughs… now and then was to be heard from the whole collection of human beings a devastating sigh.'

A reader might find him- or herself sitting next to the famous, mysterious or downright mad. A surreptitious glance at the books on which one's neighbour was working could provide a fascinating distraction from one's own research.

Generations of readers are immortalized in literature. Charles Dickens was one of the first, describing in *Sketches by Boz* (1836) the 'shabby-genteel' people who then frequented the room. For Arnold Bennett in *A Man from the North* (1898) the assorted readers comprised 'bishops, statesmen, men of science, historians, needy

'Two Ways of Studying in the Reading Room', *The Graphic*, 15 January 1887

21

pedants, popular authors whose broughams are waiting in the precincts, journalists, medical students, law students, curates, hack-writers, women with clipped hair and black aprons, idlers; all short-sighted and all silent.'

In *The End of the Affair* (1958) Graham Greene remarks on 'the dusty inmates of the reading room – the men who wore hats and scarves indoors for warmth, the Indian who was painfully studying the complete works of George Eliot, or the man who slept every day with his head laid beside the same pile of books.' Somewhat irreverently David Lodge, in *The British Museum is Falling Down* (1965), describes the Reading Room in winter as a 'refuge for scholars, post-graduates and other bums and layabouts in search of a warm seat'.

Romance flourished or died among the catalogue desks, where impromptu conversations could be launched with strangers, to be followed by closer acquaintance in the dingy Museum tearoom or one of the neighbouring cafés. In the 1870s and 1880s Samuel Butler sitting at B.16, had for many years a platonic relationship with the importunate Miss Eliza Mary Ann Savage in Row G, writing two sonnets after her death, confessing that by failing to respond to her friendship he had 'loved too wisely but not well'. Both Eleanor Marx and her lover Edward Aveling had reader's tickets. The Museum's index card with details of Eleanor's ticket is laconically annotated 'suicide Apr. 1898'. Persuaded into a suicide pact by Aveling, Eleanor killed herself and he survived free to pursue other affairs.

In Victorian times the clergy were much in evidence, some finding it more convenient to copy old sermons than compose new ones, the more unscrupulous occasionally dispensing with copying and surreptitiously removing sermons wholesale. The more blatant of the Victorian idlers with their daily newspapers were discouraged when in 1861 the Trustees directed that these could not be read in the Reading Room. The novel-readers were similarly dissuaded when in 1889 novels less than five years old were no longer issued.

Readers discovered breaking the rules were reported to the Trustees (the Museum's governing body) and for many years a black book with the names of those banned from the Reading Room was maintained. Among the odder grounds for expulsion recalled by the staff were 'strange behaviour at King's Lynn' and 'using a reader's ticket as a handkerchief'. Fighting in the Reading Room was relatively common, together with begging and uncleanliness. One protagonist argued indignantly that, as a real writer, he should not be penalised since he had only been exchanging blows with a hack journalist.

Once a year during 'closed week' readers were banished from the Room to wander aimlessly around the Museum and surrounding streets, as desks were repolished, carpets cleaned and books checked, and those which had been mislaid once more reappeared.

Writers and the Reading Room

In the centre of the reading-room at the British Museum sit four men fenced about by a quadruple ring of unwieldy volumes which are an index to all the knowledge in the world… Vague, reverberating noises roll heavily from time to time across the chamber, but no one looks up; the incessant cannibal feast of the living upon the dead goes speechlessly forward, the trucks of food are always moving to and fro, and the nonchalant waiters seem to take no rest

Arnold Bennett, *A Man from the North* (1898)

The playwright G B Shaw used the Reading Room at the beginning of his career. Pen and ink drawing by Harry Furniss

William Makepeace Thackeray wrote 'I have seen all sorts of domes… and have been struck by none of them so much as by that catholic dome in Bloomsbury'. Oil on canvas by Frank Stone c 1839

Although the Reading Room attracted all sorts of humanity, the largest group of users was undoubtedly those who made their living by writing in some form or other, succinctly described as 'novelists in search of plots, historians in search of facts, and critics in search of mistakes', one generation, as Arnold Bennett noted above, providing ideas for the next to exploit, as endless barrows of books were trundled to and from the Sorting Passage. In some instances the only trace of their presence is to be found in the index cards, registers or signature books (where they assert that they are over 21 and pledge to obey the Museum's rules), glimpses of others do, however, exist in diaries or biographies.

Some like Robert Frost who obtained a temporary ticket in 1912 or Stevie Smith in 1924 paid very fleeting visits. Others were to be seen there at the beginning of their careers. Charles Dickens was a frequent visitor to the old reading room in the 1830s when studying to be a shorthand reporter, declaring later that his time in the Museum was the 'usefulest' to himself he had ever passed. The playwright George Bernard Shaw wrote of his daily visits to the Reading Room for about eight years when he first arrived in London, 'Oh (if I may quote Wordsworth) the difference to me!' He expressed his gratitude towards the end of his life by appointing the Museum a third residuary legatee of his will.

Some came briefly for specific purposes: George Eliot was there in the 1860s carrying out background research for *Romola* and *Felix Holt*.

A number haunted the room for many years: G M Trevelyan in his life of the great historian Lord Macaulay writes that Macaulay was privileged for 'his habit was to work in the King's Library… He did his writing at one of the oak tables which stand in the centre of the room, sitting away from the wall for the sake of the light.'

Samuel Butler, author of *Erewhon* records that he spent years removing the little-read Frost's *Lives of Eminent Christians* from the reference shelves, only able to work by propping up his blotting pad against it to form a slanting desk. Butler successfully petitioned for the return of this otherwise unconsulted book when it was withdrawn to storage by the staff. George Gissing was one of the regular readers, writing in the semi-autobiographical *The Private Papers of Henry*

Oscar Wilde, whose ticket was withdrawn after his conviction and imprisonment. Albumen panel portrait print by Napoleon Sarony 1882

Rycroft (1902) that 'At the time when I was literally starving in London, when it seemed impossible that I should ever gain a living from my own pen, how many days have I spent at the British Museum, reading as disinterestedly as if I had been without a care!'

George Orwell, author of *Nineteen Eighty Four* came twice, first in 1928 on his return from living rough in Paris and again in 1937 after fighting in the Spanish Civil War. Graham Greene obtained a ticket in 1930 when working on a biography of the Earl of Rochester. In 1920 the detective-story writer Dorothy L Sayers gained admission to work on a PhD thesis on 'The Permanent Elements in Popular Heroic Fiction with a Special Study of Modern Criminological Romance', but soon turned to the more popular Peter Wimsey series, the first of which was published in 1923.

Some prominent readers found the Museum rather daunting: in July 1868 the poet, A C Swinburne, overcome by the atmosphere, and no doubt his dissolute life, startled readers in his row by collapsing over his desk and grazing his forehead. Oscar Wilde was admitted in 1879 but the Trustees' Minutes record the withdrawal of his reader's ticket in 1895 following his imprisonment for homosexual practices. Another poet, W B Yeats, compiling an anthology of Irish fairy-stories, recalls in his autobiography that he must have been delicate at the time (1887) for he put off for hour after hour consulting a book because he could not face lifting the heavy volumes of the catalogues.

Thackeray in his diary wrote eloquently: 'In the great circle of the library Time is looking in to Space'. Matthew Arnold hails 'that delightful spot, that Happy Island in Bloomsbury, the Reading Room of the British Museum'. More prosaically the children's illustrator Beatrix Potter remarks to a young admirer in 1903, 'I went to the Reading Room at the British Museum this morning to see a delightful old book full of rhymes... There were not many people, but some of them were very funny'.

Angus Wilson in 1966 photographed by Philippe Halsman

Others, including Edmund Gosse and Angus Wilson, were Museum employees. Margaret Drabble in her biography of the author Angus Wilson, Deputy Superintendent from 1951, gives a portrait of him presiding over the centre desk 'a colourful bird in a vast circular cage, bow-tied, blue-rinsed, chattering loudly to readers and staff and friends on the telephone... and confidently offering advice or even reading manuscripts or proofs for students, displaced Americans, Polish refugees, crazy scholars, and aspiring novelists'.

The Reading Room in fiction

Given the bizarre nature of some readers it is not surprising that the line between fact and fiction became blurred. Not only Conan Doyle but also Sherlock Holmes had a reader's ticket. In *The Musgrave Ritual* (1894) Holmes remarks that when he first came up to London he had rooms in Montague Street, just round the corner from the British

Alfred Hitchcock's 1929 film *Blackmail* concludes with a perilous chase across the dome of the Reading Room

Museum, and there he 'waited, filling in my too abundant leisure time by studying all those branches of science which might make me more efficient'. A later writer, W S Baring-Gould, (*Sherlock Holmes: A Biography* (1962)) describes an imaginary meeting between Holmes and Karl Marx: 'A fat man with a large brown beard looked up from his statistics of the minute wages earned in the Lancashire cotton industry, and noticed Holmes' peculiar line of reading. "You are interested in assassination?" he asked in a thick Prussian accent. "Yes", Holmes admitted. "Then you must meet my friends the Anarchists."'

Many of the writers who spent time in the Reading Room used it as a setting for their novels. E M Forster's Ansell in *The Longest Journey* (1907) viewed it with affection: 'Ansell was in his favourite haunt – the reading-room of the British Museum. In that book-encircled space he always could find peace. He loved to see the volumes rising tier above tier into the misty dome. He loved the chairs that glide so noiselessly, and the radiating desks, and the central area, where the catalogue shelves curve round the Superintendent's throne. There he knew that his life was not ignoble. It was worth while to grow old and dusty seeking for truth though truth is unattainable, restating questions that have been stated at the beginning of the world.'

George Gissing whose novel *New Grub Street* provides a portrait of the Reading Room in the 1880s

By contrast George Gissing writes in *New Grub Street* (1891) of the desperation of the poor scholars like himself. His impecunious copyist Marian Yule, who sits in the November fog, sees the Reading Room as hell: 'The fog grew thicker; she looked up at the windows beneath the dome and saw that they were a dusky yellow. Then her eye discerned an official walking along the upper gallery, and in pursuance of her grotesque humour, her mocking misery, she likened him to a black, lost soul, doomed to wander in an eternity of vain research along endless shelves. Or again, the readers who sat here at these radiating lines of desks, what were they but hapless flies caught in a huge web, its nucleus the great circle of the Catalogue?'

Virginia Woolf's description of Miss Marchmont in *Jacob's Room* is reminiscent of many real, somewhat eccentric readers, for example Miss McDonald, normally dressed in Bermuda shorts and a cape, fondly remembered by generations of readers, who cycled to Bloomsbury daily for nearly 50 years to be first in the queue for entry to the Reading Room, researching no-one knew what, and publishing nothing. Woolf writes: 'What was she seeking through millions of pages, in her old plush dress, and her wig of claret-coloured hair, with her gems and her chilblains? Sometimes one thing, sometimes another, to confirm her philosophy that colour is sound – or, perhaps, it has something to do with music. She could never quite say, though it was not for lack of trying.'

In a fanciful piece in his *Notebooks* Butler gave his explanation of how the windows of the dome were cleaned: 'Once a year or so the figures on the Assyrian bas-reliefs break adrift and may be seen, with their scaling ladders and all, cleaning the outside of the windows in the dome of the reading room. It is very pretty to watch them and they would photograph beautifully. If I live to see them do it again I must certainly snapshot them. You can see them smoking and sparring and this year they have left a little hole in the window above the clock.'

Virginia Woolf's *Jacob's Room* is set in the Reading Room around the turn of the century. Platinum print by George Charles Beresford 1902

Fictional characters pursued various forms of research: for example in Thomas Hardy's *Tess of the d'Urbervilles* (1891) the rich tradesman Mr Simon Stoke peruses 'the pages of works devoted to extinct, half-extinct, obscured, and ruined families appertaining to the quarter of England in which he proposed to settle', and decides that d'Urberville looked and sounded as well as any of them and accordingly annexes it to his own name.

Using the Reading Room was not without hazard. Bram Stoker's Jonathan Harker in *Dracula* (1897) *en route* to Transylvania, unaware of the horror to come and having time to spare in London, searches amongst the books and maps but is unable to find the exact location of Castle Dracula. The narrator in Jerome K Jerome's *Three Men in a Boat* walks in to check on the treatment for 'some slight ailment' and, having consulted a medical encyclopaedia crawls out a decrepit wreck, convinced he had everything between A and Z but housemaid's knee. Alfred Hitchcock's 1929 film *Blackmail* concludes with a gripping chase across the exterior of the dome. David Lodge's anxious graduate student in *The British Museum is Falling Down* (1965) after a series of misadventures loses himself in the bookstacks 'a dark, underworld, heavy with the odour of decaying paper'. For Frederick Forsyth's nameless assassin in *The Day of the Jackal* (1971) it is an admirable place in which to research locations for murder.

Although the Reading Room has not inspired a vast outpouring of verse, some of the poets who read there have left fragments. There is a rather cloying piece by Rose Macaulay which begins 'Soaked in the stream of a honey-coloured dream lies a wheel that turns not round'.

The best and most serious is *The British Museum Reading Room* by Louis MacNeice who caught the anxious atmosphere in 1939:

Under the hive-like dome the stooping haunted readers
Go up and down the alleys, tap the cells of knowledge
…Cranks, hacks, poverty-stricken scholars…
Hanging like bats in a world of inverted values,
Folded up in themselves in a world which is safe and silent…

… Between the enormous fluted Ionic columns
There seeps from heavily jowled or hawk-like foreign faces
The guttural sorrow of the refugees

William Plomer in *A Ticket for the Reading-Room* (1929) is less respectful, picturing a typical reader:

On he shuffles, quietly mumbling
Figures, facts and formulae –
Bats are busy in the belfry,
In the bonnet hums a bee

At the Reading Room he settles
Pince-nez on his bottle nose,
Reads and scribbles, reads and scribbles,
Till the day draws to a close

Readers at the central catalogue desks 1933. The lampshades were introduced in 1893

The Reading Room and revolution

From the 1857 Reading Room and its predecessors were to emerge ideas and movements which would change the world. Hall Caine described the revolutionaries in *The Eternal City* (1901): 'A shabby coat here, a shiny hat there, a quaint figure over yonder. Dreaming dreams they are never to see realised, living on, hoping, buoying themselves up with visions.'

Karl Marx used the Reading Room daily for almost 30 years. Photo gravure c 1870

The political system with its deepest roots in the Reading Room is Communism. Karl Marx (1818–83) was first admitted to the old reading room in June 1850 and obtained the last renewal of his ticket in November 1877. He worked there on a number of projects including *Das Kapital*, the first volume of which appeared in German in 1867. Although many readers had favourite desks, it is not known exactly where Marx sat since seats could not be reserved in advance, but the assumption is that he would have occupied a seat in rows K to P near to the historical reference books he would have used. The German Social Democrat Wilhelm Liebknecht (1826–1900), who knew Marx in London, wrote in his biographical memoir: 'About this time the magnificent reading room of the British Museum, with its inexhaustible treasures of books, had been built – and thither, where he passed a certain time every day, Marx drove us. To learn! To learn!… While the rest of the fugitives were laying plans for the overthrow of the world and intoxicating themselves day by day, evening by evening, with the hasheesh-drink of "Tomorrow it will start!" – we… were sitting in the British Museum and trying to educate ourselves and to prepare arms and ammunition for the battles of the future… Sometimes we would not have had a bite, but that would not prevent our going to the Museum – there were at least comfortable chairs to sit down on and in winter a cheering warmth – which were missing at home, if one had any "house" or "home" at all.'

Smoking being forbidden in the Reading Room, it is not unlikely that Marx joined the furtive smokers on the Colonnade for Liebknecht writes that he was a passionate smoker who had discovered a source of particularly 'cheap and nasty' cigars on his way through Holborn.

Other revolutionary thinkers and activists included the anarchist Prince Peter Kropotkin (1842–1921) who obtained a ticket in 1881. The 'father of Russian Marxism', Georgi Valentinovich Plekhanov (1857–1918) gained admission in 1894. Vladimir Ilyich Lenin (1870–1924) applied for a reader's ticket under the alias Jacob Richter in 1902 in order to study 'the land question' and a renewal under his own name Oulianoff in 1908 to research 'comparatively new English and new German philosophy'. He is said to have used the Library

Vladimir Ilyich Lenin obtained a reader's ticket in 1902 and 1908. Photo 1918

whenever he was in London and may, therefore, have adopted further undiscovered identities. Lenin may have frequented rows G, H, R or L, the latter being the most likely as it was opposite reference works on British and European history.

Lenin arranged for Leon Trotsky (1879–1940) to obtain a ticket in 1902 or 1903 under an as yet unknown alias. Trotsky wrote in his memoirs that he was insatiable and 'gorged himself' on the books. The exiled Vera Zasulich who had shot and wounded the Governor of St Petersburg spent time researching a book on Rousseau, describing in letters to friends how she could only find peace of mind in the Museum, where, although it could be terribly stuffy at times, she did not mind because she buried herself up to her ears in piles of books and found she was gradually overcoming her desire to dash out every hour for a cigarette.

The poet Sergei Kravchinsky who was said to have assassinated the St Petersburg Chief of Police was another reader, having registered under the name of 'Sergius Stepniak', and struck up an acquaintance with the daughter of the Keeper of Printed Books, the diarist Olive Garnett. Stepniak used to horrify the Garnett family by carrying books out of the Reading Room at lunchtime but insisted this was not a crime because he always took them back. Another reader was L Martov (1873–1923) the pseudonym of I O Tsederbaum, one of the leaders of the Menshevik party. The Russian emigrés tended to use complex aliases, which even today makes it difficult to trace their movements, a not unreasonable precaution since the Tsar's secret police operated in London, and they were also under surveillance by the British police who arrested one emigré at the exit from the Reading Room in 1897 for soliciting the murder of the Tsar.

Perhaps not surprisingly, the Museum Trustees at this time withdrew the second edition of Cundall's *Dictionary of Explosives* and ordered that it not be included in the *Catalogue*.

Leon Trotsky, Tsarist police photograph 1897 a few years before his escape to London

Lenin's 1902 application for a reader's ticket to study 'the land question'

The British Library

A date which has been in the diary longer than most

Her Majesty The Queen on the opening of the new British Library building at St Pancras,
25 June 1998

For many years, as the Museum's collections grew, there were
proposals to enlarge the building or to rehouse objects elsewhere.
Natural history was moved to South Kensington (now the Natural
History Museum) in the 1880s. This temporary alleviation of the
perennial space problem did not last and after the Second World War
measures were taken to secure the site to the south of Great Russell
Street. In August 1962 two architects, Leslie Martin and Colin St John
Wilson, were appointed to prepare plans for a new building. The old
buildings south of the Museum were to be flattened but in their place
would have appeared a central pedestrian piazza running from the
Museum to St George's Church, an underground car-park, a new
library on the east side, a new lecture theatre, exhibition building and
restaurant on the west, with shops, offices and flats.

Humanities Reading Room
at the new British Library,
St Pancras. Architect Sir
Colin St John Wilson

Plans were drawn and redrawn. Eventually, in 1972 the British
Library, a new organisation separate from the Museum, but
incorporating the Museum's library departments and other libraries
was established by Act of Parliament and came into being in July 1973
on the assumption that it would remain in the vicinity. In 1974,
however, it became apparent that the local authority, the Borough
of Camden, was determined on conservation grounds to oppose the
new building. In December the Government announced that the
new library would be located next to St Pancras railway station.
This marked the end of the old Reading Room. In 1982 the foundation
stone was laid for the new library building designed by Sir Colin
St John Wilson. It was completed in July 1997 and formally opened
by The Queen on 25 June 1998.

The British Library's transfer to St Pancras represents the biggest
move of books and library services the world has ever seen. It began
in December 1996 and was completed in June 1999 when the last of
12 million books arrived. About 153 miles (245 km) of shelf space of
monographs and periodicals were moved, plus substantial amounts
of non-book items. The target rate for the general humanities stock
was 300yd (300m) or about 10,000 books per day. Just over 43 miles
(70km) of humanities stock was moved, in addition there were 13
miles (22km) of rare books, nearly 2 miles (3km) of music, 5 miles
(8.5km) of manuscripts, plus map and philatelic collections.

The Reading Room at Bloomsbury closed on 25 October 1997, as
it had opened in 1857, with a champagne party on the catalogue desks.

The new Reading Room

…the fire-work gasp factor of the famous… Reading Room
Christopher Logue, *Prince Charming: a Memoir* (1999)

Previous page: The Great Court under construction, looking north towards Senate House. The original London brick facing of the Reading Room can be seen, it is now concealed by Spanish limestone

Nothing can ever quite prepare the first-time visitor for the experience of entering the Reading Room and familiarity does not entirely diminish the initial sense of awe. The soaring dome is higher than it appears in photographs, the gilding more rich, the azure blue more overpowering, the muted sounds have a distinct character. These are the same desks where Marx drafted *Capital* and where hundreds of thousands of readers from all over the world studied and dreamed. Today we are privileged to see it as it was for only a decade or so after its opening in 1857, before Victorian fogs dulled the gilding and deposited grime over the azure blue of the dome.

The new Reading Room is part of the Queen Elizabeth II Great Court on which work began in March 1998. Considerable skill and ingenuity were involved in restoring this great interior to its original splendour. The papier mâché lining the dome was found to have shrunk, causing a network of cracks. An innovative repair method was devised, inspired by the Royal Navy's mix of hemp and caulk used to waterproof wooden ships. The cracks were first loose-filled with cotton wadding. One and a half miles (2.4km) of Flexiweave, a material similar to surgical bandage, was applied across the cracks and the edges blended to the surface with a filler. An unconventional zero tension Swiss oil-based paint sits on top of the fabric, rather than being partially absorbed by the material. This allows the cracks to move beneath the newly applied paintwork.

The roof of the Great Court and the Reading Room dome provide a new London landmark Opposite: Designed by Sydney Smirke the cool, light tint of the dome contrasts with the rich warm tones of the books

The original colour scheme, which had vanished beneath later
repaintings, was recreated using photographs and a sample of the
original paint from the Museum's archives, and evidence revealed
by cross-sections of paint layers. Using solvents and scalpels, the
thick obscuring overpaint was painstakingly reduced down to the
fragile outlines of the first decoration. The restoration required
15½ miles (25km) of sheets of 23.25 carat gold leaf and over
2 tonnes of paints.

The outside of the Reading Room, which was not intended to
be seen by visitors, was constructed of rather undistinguished yellow
London brick and was in any case obscured by the bookstacks. It has
now been faced with Spanish limestone (*Galicia Capri*).

New uses have been found for the Reading Room. In the
Walter and Leonore Annenberg Centre the terminals of COMPASS
(Collections Multimedia Public Access System) provide access for
visitors of all ages to a database of the Museum's collections linked
to a sophisticated search facility. Users can now browse through
images of thousands of objects, finding out more about them,
the cultures in which they originated, and also compiling their own
tours of the Museum.

A generous donation from the Paul Hamlyn Foundation has
enabled the Museum to set up a public reference library which will
eventually consist of some 25,000 volumes. It is open to all, providing
information about the civilizations, cultures and societies represented
in the British Museum collections. It complements COMPASS by
making available, wherever possible, those books listed in connection
with the selected objects. The vast range of subjects extends from
ancient history and archaeology to body adornment and jewellery,
and, like the Museum, covers most of the world.

The books are arranged by subject on open-access shelving
around the Reading Room. Children are catered for with a separate
section of low shelves in the centre. On-line catalogues are available
to help locate the books and staff are on hand to provide assistance.

The Paul Hamlyn Library is unique in its access and scope,
providing an invaluable resource for those wishing to explore the
Museum's collections in greater depth.

In the public viewing area of the Reading Room is an exhibition of
books written by authors linked with the Reading Room. Here Beatrix
Potter's *The Tale of Peter Rabbit* is shelved with Karl Marx's *Capital*,
Len Deighton's *Funeral in Berlin* with Charles Dickens's *Sketches
by Boz*, M R James's *Collected Ghost Stories* with Charles Kingsley's

Left: Each reader's place
is numbered. Row A was
originally reserved for
lady readers
Right: A reader's desk
with fold-out book rest
and hooks for pens

Decorative grille at the
end of a row of desks
Following page: The
interplay of reflections
in the Great Court. The
outline of Lord Foster's
steel and glass roof is
set against Sydney
Smirke's gilded dome

Water Babies, V I Lenin's *Collected Works* with the poems of Ted
Hughes, Baroness Orczy's *The Scarlet Pimpernel* with Anthony
Powell's *Agents and Patients*, an indication of the vast and varied
output of those who used the British Museum Reading Room and
its library. On the two upper levels inside the dome are shelved books
from the Museum's ethnographical library which includes the library
of the Royal Anthropological Institute.

The new Reading Room was opened by Her Majesty The Queen,
on 6 December 2000. When it was first unveiled a century and a half
earlier *The Leisure Hour* hailed it as 'a building which men of science
will come far to see, and which may be the admiration of generations
yet unborn'. That remains true today.

Facts and figures

- the inner courtyard (now the Great Court) measures 313ft (95.4m) by 235ft (71.6m)

- the Reading Room and bookstacks take up a total groundspace of 258ft (78.6m) by 184ft (56.1m), c 21% of the courtyard

- the Reading Room does not form an exact circle since the east-west dimension is some 1½in (40mm) longer than the north-south dimension

- the dome of the Reading Room is 140ft (43m) in diameter and 106ft (32.3m) in height – only 2ft (0.6m) less in diameter than the world's largest domed building, the Pantheon in Rome

- surpassing the Pantheon in ingenuity of construction, the dome is supported by 20 iron ribs each having a sectional area of 10ft^2 (0.93m^2) including the brick casing, or 200ft^2 (18.6m^2) in all, whereas the ribs of the Pantheon occupy over 7,400ft^2 (687.5m^2)

- about 4,200 tons (4,267 tonnes) of the materials were used in the dome, or upwards of 200 tons (203.2 tonnes) on each rib

- the glazed 'lantern' of the dome is 40ft (12.9m) in diameter

- the 20 circular-headed windows, 27ft (8.2m) high by 12ft (3.7m) wide, are inserted at equal intervals, 35ft (10.7m) from the ground

- the doors on the east and west sides are later additions

- the floor area is 14,500ft^2 (1,350m^2), with 1,250,000ft^3 (35,375m^3) of space

At the end of the day the last reader is evicted by staff with lanterns. *The Graphic*, 15 January 1887

- the floor was covered with 'kamptulicon', a Victorian mixture of rubber, gutta percha and cork on a canvas backing, to reduce noise (now replaced by carpet)

- the tables for readers radiate out from the keyhole-shaped catalogue desk like a spider's web

- there were originally 302 places for readers at 19 long tables (of which A and T were at first reserved for ladies, but little used), plus 16 small tables with book-rests for readers wishing to consult very large volumes

- the number of places was increased in the 1880s with the provision of extra furniture (now removed)

- a double row of seats opposite the entrance was replaced in the 1950s by an enquiry desk and cabinets for catalogue cards (now removed to provide a viewing area)

- a reader's working desk space measured 4ft 3in (1.3m) long and 2ft 1in (0.6m) deep, with a shelf for books or case, a hat-peg under the desk, a book rest, and, at one time, pen, ink and bristles on which to rest the wet pen nib

- three types of mahogany chair were provided, with seats of polished wood, padded leather (the most popular) or wicker

- the desks were originally covered in black leather – the blue covering and chairs now in use date from the 1960s

- 80,000 books were stored within the Room on three tiers of shelving, 24,000 of them were available for reference on the ground floor

- there is a BBC recording entitled 'The Silence in the British Museum Reading Room'

Right: The Reading Room as it might have been. Artist's impression 1857 (*Illustrated London News*) showing statues and a flamboyant decorative scheme which were never executed
Far right: 'Tottering under the weight of knowledge'. G Lawson c 1890

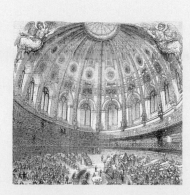

Notable readers

Peter Ackroyd (1949–)
Matthew Arnold (1822–88)
Charles Babbage (1792–1871)
Robert Baden-Powell (1857–1941)
Walter Bagehot (1826–77)
Cecil Beaton (1904–80)
Samuel Beckett (1906–89)
Max Beerbohm (1872–1956)
Hilaire Belloc (1870–1953)
Arnold Bennett (1867–1931)
Harrison Birtwistle (1934–)
R D Blackmore (1825–1900)
Louis Blanc (1811–82)
Arthur Bliss (1891–1975)
Malcolm Bradbury (1932–2000)
Asa Briggs (1921–)
Rupert Brooke (1887–1915)
Robert Browning (1812–89)
Edward Burne-Jones (1833–98)
Samuel Butler (1835–1902)
A S Byatt (1936–)
Thomas Carlyle (1795–1881)
G K Chesterton (1874–1936)
Wilkie Collins (1824–89)
Joseph Conrad (1857–1924)
George Cruikshank (1792–1878)
Charles Darwin (1809–92)
Len Deighton (1929–)
Charles Dickens (1812–70)
Benjamin Disraeli (1804–81)

Arthur Conan Doyle (1859–1930)
Margaret Drabble (1939–)
Isadora Duncan (1878–1927)
Lawrence Durrell (1912–90)
Edward Elgar (1857–1934)
George Eliot (1819–80)
T S Eliot (1888–1965)
Jacob Epstein (1880–1959)
Michael Faraday (1791–1867)
M R D Foot (1918–)
Ford Madox Ford (1873–1939)
C S Forester (1899–1966)
E M Forster (1879–1970)
Antonia Fraser (1932–)
Robert Frost (1874–1963)
John Galsworthy (1867–1933)
Elizabeth Gaskell (1810–65)
W S Gilbert (1836–1911)
Ernst Gombrich (1909–)
Graham Greene (1904–91)
Germaine Greer (1939–)
H Rider Haggard (1856–1925)
Thomas Hardy (1840–1928)
Eric Hobsbawm (1917–)
Michael Holroyd (1935–)
Gustav Holst (1874–1934)
Ted Hughes (1930–98)
Aldous Huxley (1894–1963)
T H Huxley (1825–95)
M R James (1862–1936)
Jerome K Jerome (1859–1927)
Ruth Prawer Jhabvala (1927–)
H R F Keating (1926–)

Arnold Bennett

A S Byatt

T S Eliot

John Maynard Keynes
(1883–1946)
Charles Kingsley (1819–75)
Rudyard Kipling (1865–1936)
Edwin Landseer (1802–73)
John Le Carré (1931–)
V I Lenin (1870–1924)
Peter Levi (1931–)
David Lodge (1935–)
Christopher Logue (1926–)
Lord Macaulay (1800–59)
Karl Marx (1818–83)
George Meredith (1828–1909)
John Millais (1829–96)
Patrick Moore (1923–)
V S Naipaul (1932–)
Conor Cruise O'Brien (1917–)
Iona (1923–) & Peter
(1918–82) Opie
Baroness Orczy (1865–1947)
George Orwell (1903–50)
Sylvia Pankhurst (1882–1960)
Nikolaus Pevsner (1902–83)
Beatrix Potter (1866–1943)
Ezra Pound (1885–1972)
Anthony Powell (1905–2000)
Christina Rossetti (1830–94)
Dante Gabriel Rossetti (1828–82)
John Ruskin (1819–1900)
Bertrand Russell (1872–1970)
Dorothy L Sayers (1893–1957)
G B Shaw (1856–1950)
Alan Sillitoe (1928–)

W Somerset Maugham
(1874–1965)
Muriel Spark (1918–)
Gertrude Stein (1874–1946)
Bram Stoker (1847–1912)
Marie Stopes (1880–1958)
Algernon Charles Swinburne
(1837–1909)
A J P Taylor (1906–90)
Alfred, Lord Tennyson (1809–92)
William Makepeace Thackeray
(1811–63)
Colin Thubron (1939–)
G M Trevelyan (1876–1962)
Hugh Trevor-Roper (1914–)
Anthony Trollope (1815–82)
Leon Trotsky (1879–1940)
Mark Twain (1835–1910)
John Updike (1932–)
Ralph Vaughan Williams
(1872–1958)
Evelyn Waugh (1903–66)
H G Wells (1866–1946)
Oscar Wilde (1854–1900)
Virginia Woolf (1882–1941)
W B Yeats (1865–1939)

Dorothy L Sayers

Anthony Powell

H G Wells

Books about the Reading Room

G F Barwick, *The Reading Room of the British Museum*, London 1929
P R Harris, *The Reading Room*, London 1986
J Penn (pseudonym), *For Readers Only*, New York 1937

For Russian emigrés and the Reading Room see R Henderson, 'Lenin and the British Museum Library', *Solanus*, n.s. 4, 1990, 3–15; ibid 'Russian political emigrés and the British Museum Library', *Library History*, 9, 1 and 2, 1991, 59–68

For a selection of references to the Reading Room in literature see:
E F Ellis, *The British Museum in Fiction*, Buffalo 1981

Books about The British Museum and its library

R G W Anderson, *The Great Court and the British Museum*, London 2000
M Caygill, *The Story of the British Museum*, London 1998
M Caygill and C Date, *Building the British Museum*, London 1999
R Cowtan, *Memories of the British Museum*, London 1872
J Mordaunt Crook, *The British Museum: a case-study in architectural politics*, London 1972
E Edwards, *Lives of the Founders, and Notes of the Chief Benefactors and Organisers of the British Museum,* London 1870, repr 1969
A Esdaile, *The British Museum Library*, London 1946
P R Harris, *A History of the British Museum Library 1753–1973*, London 1998
E Miller, *That Noble Cabinet*, London 1973
E Miller, *Prince of Librarians. The life and times of Antonio Panizzi*, London 1967

Acknowledgements

Particular thanks are due to the Editor of this book, Josephine Turquet, without whom it would not have been achieved. The support for the project by Carol Homden is also gratefully acknowledged. Christopher Date, Pam Smith, Gillian Hughes, Sat Jandu, Philip Attwood, Simon Tutty and Dudley Hubbard of The British Museum have also contributed. P R Harris, lately of the British Library, has offered his expertise, as has David Mitchell, and John Hopson Archivist of the British Library. We are most grateful to Mrs Margaret Warner, a descendant of Sydney Smirke, for her generosity in allowing us to use his photograph.

The British Museum wishes to thank the following for their contributions to the Reading Room:
Walter and Leonore Annenberg
The Paul Hamlyn Foundation

Production Editor:
J Turquet
Department of Marketing and Public Affairs, The British Museum
Design:
Esterson Lackersteen
Print:
Perivan

© 2000 The Trustees of The British Museum

ISBN 0 86159 985 3

Photographic credits and copyrights:
The Trustees of The British Museum 2–3, 5–6, 8–10, 12–16, 18–23, 30, 32–33, 44–45 (Photos: Dudley Hubbard 32–33)
The British Library Board 28, 31
Canal+ Image UK Ltd (*Blackmail*) 26
Mary Evans Picture Library (Gissing) 26
Mark Gerson (Byatt) 46
Photo © Philippe Halsman (Wilson) 25

David King Collection (Lenin and Trotsky) 30
By courtesy of the National Portrait Gallery, London 24–25, 27, 46–47
Phil Sayer cover, 34–42
Sports and General Press Agency 17
Mrs Margaret Warner 7